Copyright ℕ

MW01278518

Copyright © 2012 by Charlie Valentino. All Rights Reserved.

Reproduction or translation of any part of this work beyond that permitted by section 107 or 108 of the 1976 United States Copyright Act without permission of the copyright owner is unlawful. Requests for permission or further information should be addressed to the author.

Charlie Valentino
UK

This publication is designed to provide accurate and authoritative information in regard to the subject matter covered. It is sold the understanding that the publisher is not engaged in rendering legal, accounting, or other professional services. If legal advice or other expert assistance is required, the services of a competent professional person should be sought.

First Printing, 2012

ISBN-13: 978-1475025972
ISBN-10: 1475025971

Printed in the United States of America

*"The only way to expand your comfort zone
is to live outside it!"*

Charlie Valentino

Table Of Contents

Section 1

The Pep Talk

Introduction

Thank you for picking up your copy of Confidence For Men by me, Charlie Valentino. It means an awful lot that you've put your faith in me to help you out with what is a major problem for many men around the world, of all ages and from all walks of life. I hope to repay that faith ten fold by giving you the knowledge and tools to overcome this problem and enable you to improve your life.

However, paying money to read a book is one thing, but putting what you learn into practice and actually making the positive changes needed to change your life for the better is another thing entirely.

For a long time I worked as a personal trainer in a gym. It used to amaze me just how many people thought they could get fit simply by paying their hard earned money to join the gym, and then never actually, or hardly ever turning up for a workout.

What you're about to learn will work! It will work extremely well and it will change your life. But you have to promise you're not going to be like those gym clients and make excuses not to put in the hard work. Knowledge is the most powerful force in the world! But it's nothing without action! You have to act on what you learn in this book.

You probably want to know just who I am and what makes me so qualified to teach you about building confidence to change your life. Well I'll take this opportunity to tell you a little bit about myself.

You see, I was always the guy at school who nobody ever noticed. I faded into the background trying to get through each day with as little fuss as possible. It's no wonder few people remember me. When I went to college, one of the lecturers actually made a comment that I used my hair to cover up my face so I didn't have to look at anybody. I was the same as any other guy, I wanted girls to like me and I wanted to be successful, but I always assumed success would just come and I wouldn't have to put any hard work in to get it. The years ticked by and I was still very nervous in peoples company. I could only ever get into decent conversations with my family or closest friends, of whom there wasn't many.

Things started to change for me in my mid twenties when I started university and I started to put myself out there a little more. Some of the things I did were crazy, and those are the things I remember the most and that changed me the most.

I admit I'm a natural introvert and I'm proud of that because it puts me in a position to be able to teach confidence to men from a position you can hopefully all relate to. I have no qualifications to be able to teach this, only my own experiences and what I know works very well.

I wanted to become more confident mainly so that girls would like me more. We all know that confidence is one of the main things, if not the number one thing that girls are attracted to in men. I assume this was a major motivator for you in picking up this book.

However, confidence is also a much valued trait in the workplace. Companies always promote their most confident individuals ahead of the rest as it's confident men and women that can drive their ideas forward the most effective, pick up new clients and overall help to bring in more money for the company.

Confident men always look and seem happier than their shy counterparts too. And when it's all said and done, happiness is the name of the game and what we all strive for.

What Is Confidence?

The dictionary defines confidence as:

"belief in oneself and one's powers or abilities"

Read that a couple more times!

So what would happen if you took that guy who was really confident around the workplace and put him in a situation that was completely alien to him? Would he still be confident? What if this alien situation was something you were really good at for example, something like playing the guitar or speaking a foreign language or going on a 12 mile run? Who would be the most confident guy out of the two of you in this certain situation?

It would be you!

And why is that?

It's because you are the competent one in that situation, whereas he is not!

"Competence = Confidence!"

Sure your office mate who can't run 12 miles may be great around people in the office or he may be really confident around women and that is what you want too. But you have to realize the reason

4

why he's so confident in those situations is because he's competent in them.

He's been getting into situations where he speaks to lots of different people his whole life, whereas you haven't. He's been used to speaking to large groups, many containing pretty girls and he's messed up and he moved on from it. These days he doesn't care about messing up because he's confident. But put him on a treadmill and all of a sudden, he doesn't feel so great, whereas you do because you practice running on a treadmill frequently.

I'm afraid there's no easy way to say this, but you're going to have to get competent in the area you want to become confident in. Which in this case is confidence itself! This means pushing yourself and expanding your comfort zone. This will mean you're going to have to put yourself in more and more difficult situations, where you feel completely alien, awkward and difficult. You need to acclimatise to these situations that make you feel really uncomfortable, until they no longer make you feel uncomfortable.

If expressing your opinion to a large group of people makes you feel uncomfortable and afraid, then in order to become accustomed to it, so that it no longer bothers you, then it stands to reason you're going to have to express your opinion to your group whenever the need arises.

If the thought of approaching a group of girls at college makes you sweat profusely, and trust me, I've been there, then you're going to have to do exactly that until doing just that no longer gives you the sweats.

Whatever it is you're trying to achieve, then you're going to have to get out there and do it to become good. You can't skirt round this simple basic human fact.

Like anything else, confidence has to be earned!

Here is a quote from me, I made it up myself:

"The only way to expand your comfort zone is to live outside it!"

This just happens to be very true!

If our friend from the office was to start getting on that treadmill, begin at a slow pace and run for only short distances he'd soon become competent at that. After a bit he could increase the intensity. Then he'd become competent at this new intensity. Before long he'd be at the same level you and I are and you could safely call him confident at running on a treadmill.

So if we want to improve our confidence around other people, we're going to have to become competent at it first. Sure, we can start at those low intensities, there's no harm in that, but pretty soon, we'll be wanting to go at a full sprint on the treadmill of life. That is what this book is about! I'm going to give you a huge range of techniques and strategies to push your boundaries, to get you out of your comfort zone and to change you permanently.

Sure you could pick and choose those strategies which sound the easiest or the least work to do but then obviously these would produce the least results for you. After all, if they don't test you then your head will not be forced to adapt.

It is the most basic principle of nature that we adapt to stress! The greater the stress, the greater and faster the adaptation.

This is true whether or not you're trying to lose weight at the gym, build up your muscle mass or improve your confidence.

If you do everything contained in this book then it's impossible for you not to become a more confident individual. By doing everything in this book you'll become more confident without even having to try anymore and without even knowing it. It will simply happen because you'll be the most rounded and accomplished individual you know.

So the remainder of this book will be split into two parts. The next part will focus on strategies to increase your confidence. Then the final part will give you exact ideas and tactics to employ to force this new confidence into you.

I wish you the best of luck on your journey to becoming a more confident man!

Do You Care What Other People Think Of You?

Before we get into the good stuff, I'd just like to go off on a very short tangent.

Read the title again and answer it honestly!

I'm guessing that in the vast majority of cases, the answer is a big yes! And caring too much what others think about us is a big part of what stops us from doing many of the things we really want to do.

In a way, caring what other people may or may not think about us is like being in a self-imposed prison. It cripples us literally!

When was the last time you saw a beautiful girl, wanted to talk to her but didn't because she had people around her or because there were other people nearby who might end up hearing what you were saying...heaven forbid! Or when was the last time you were in your group, had an opinion about something you wanted to tell everyone but didn't dare speak out because of that fear?

It all sounds so silly! But it's this complete irrational fear that stops many men from living their lives. We have literally locked ourselves away inside our own personal prison cell and have handed the key over to everybody else.

We could be there happily walking down the street while singing along to our iPods and then stop when we see someone come round the corner, pray to god they never heard us and then we'll start singing again the second they are gone. Why do we do this? Because we're thinking *what if this person thinks I'm crazy*? A better question should be, *why do I care? Why do I care, they are gone, I am never going to see that person again.*

Most people allow the quality of their lives be determined by the thoughts of strangers!

I want you to imagine that situation where you want to take action, where you want to give your opinion to your group about something or you want to go up to that girl and speak to her. You can feel something starting to brew in your head. You're thinking about it! You're thinking about what it will mean to voice your opinion or to make that approach. Now you're wondering exactly how you should say what you want to say. But right after that, you're wondering about any consequences of saying what you want to say, possibly what people may think about you. By this time, you're on the fence, on a knife edge trying to make the final decision about taking that necessary course of action. You're giving it too much thought! Then, finally the moment passes! Somebody else says something and the conversation goes in a different direction. Or perhaps the girl you were trying to get the courage to talk to stands up and walks out of the room.

Now how do you feel?

Do you feel terrible, like you've been robbed of an opportunity for personal growth? Or do you feel relief because in the end you didn't have to put yourself on the line? Do you feel relief because the strangers around you won't have any negative opinions about you in their heads?

Feeling either way is very common and normal. But the fact is if you want to improve your confidence, you're going to have to learn to break these cycles of inaction and instead take action. You're going to have to do the difficult things and carry on doing the difficult things until they become easy.

It is human nature to prefer doing the easy thing which is doing nothing or to carry doing what we've always been doing. But we both know that they are not viable options if we are going to improve our confidence.

And what of those strangers who were in the room when you wanted to speak to that girl? What of those people whose opinion meant so much to you at the time that it meant doing absolutely nothing? When you leave the room yourself and you go home and you're regretting that you didn't take any action, are these people going to matter squat to you? Will you even remember them? No you will not remember even the slightest minute detail about these people! But you may well for a long time remember that beautiful girl who you allowed to walk out of your life.

Looking back; was robbing yourself of the chance for personal growth really worth it?

"What you think of me is none of my business!"

Terry Cole-Whittaker

"Nothing in this world that's worth having comes easy!"

Dr Kelso – From Scrubs

http://www.youtube.com/watch?v=89xUz9 fZBXA

Section 2

Confidence Building Strategies

Dress Well

It was Shakespeare who said "The clothes maketh the man!" And this is very true!

It's hard to push ourselves out of our comfort zones when we're not looking and feeling our best. One of the major parts of looking our best is how we dress.

In fact I would say dressing well is absolutely imperative to our overall confidence at any given moment!

Remember my example above about the girl in the room that you wanted to talk to. You were thinking of reasons why you should not walk up to her and strike up a conversation. I know from my own experiences that in the majority of circumstances when I've chickened out, it's been because I didn't look my best. And this was really easy for me, because if I don't look my best then the decision of inaction is just so much more simple to make and I don't end up feeling quite so bad for doing nothing.

However, if I see this girl and I know I look great then I know I have no excuses for not taking action!

Although dressing well only really works to improve our confidence on a transient basis, if we dress well all the time then this transient or temporary basis becomes more permanent. It will become a normal fixture for us.

Dressing well can actually improve our mood and our confidence on a number of levels. You'll notice you'll get many more admiring glances from the ladies, and who doesn't like this? This always gives me a boost at any time of the day or night.

While we men find women attractive based largely on their figures, women find us guys attractive based largely on our style. This has been proven many times over in studies. Don't believe me? Just ask one of your female friends what is more important to them in a man; physical looks or style! Your style comes down to how you dress, how you're groomed and how you present yourself. Dressing well is a sign of status which is one of the main drivers of attraction in women. High status men also tend to be confident 99.99% of the time; it kind of comes with the territory.

However, it's really important that you dress in a style that suits you and is congruent with your lifestyle. You can look great and draw admiring glances by dressing either grungy, business like, classic, dramatic, trendy, gothic or bohemian...it really doesn't matter. But what does matter is that the way you dress suits your lifestyle.

Decide what your particular style is and then get some advice in that area. Pick up a few fashion magazines and start noticing what the better dressed guys out there are wearing. Find a style that you like the look of and replicate it for yourself, adding in your own little twists and quirks.

Consider getting slightly tighter fitting clothing. This accentuates the body more and is what women like to look at. The baggy look is terrible, it is out and gone. Firm fitting clothes are what is attractive. When you next go to the store, you need to try on a few different sizes to get the very best tight fit. Ever since I discovered that, I can shop at any old clothes store, buy budget clothes and still look and feel awesome. It's all about the fit.

A good rule of thumb is to aim for two different colours, or no more than three. It is of paramount importance that the colour of your shoes matches the colour of your belt. Brown shoes plus belt will go great with any jeans with a blue shade. Black will go with most colours.

You should also look into accessories. Smart shoulder man bags are all the rage these days, so I highly suggest you take a look at a few different styles. If you live in a cold city then a stylish scarf is also a really cool accessory to have. If your accessories match the colour of your shoes and belt then that will be a great advantage.

Just find a style that suits you and makes you feel alive. Having a good sense of style will more than make up for any deficiencies in the looks department. I highly recommend you invest some extensive time in this area.

As for your grooming...this really is a no brainer! Keep yourself looking well trimmed and sharp. Feel free to experiment with facial hair if this suits you. You'll find also that having a cool and trendy hairstyle is imperative to your confidence. Try visiting an experienced female hair stylist and getting her advice on what would suit your face and your style.

Eliminate Physical Confidence Killers

There is nothing quite like halitosis, regular nose bleeds or crooked teeth for destroying your confidence.

You may have read books that tell you looks don't matter, but trust me they do! Once again, looks are not everything, but they are certainly a very large piece of the overall confidence puzzle.

If you're going to be making a commitment to yourself to embark on a self-confidence improving journey then it would be foolish not to take into account all elements, and of course this will highly likely include some form of your physical self that is holding you back. Hey, no matter who you are, we all have them. But many of us work at eliminating them altogether, or by reducing them so much that they no longer kill our confidence.

If there's something there about your physical self that you really hate then it's not changing who you are as a person if you choose to "deal" with it.

When you consider all the other areas in this book to become a more confident guy, it is in fact the looks and physical attractiveness aspects that will be the easiest for many people. Depending on your starting point, this category will take the least amount of time when compared to much of the remaining advice in this book.

In some cases, it may just require a trip to the doctor or dentist. In other cases, what it will require is perhaps a small amount of financial investment. If your one physical imperfection is bad teeth for example then this will be a one off financial investment that will benefit you for the rest of your life.

By picking that one part of yourself that is and has always been causing your discomfort and eliminating it, not only are you improving your looks, you are also improving your confidence by default.

What's the point in living in this advanced century if we cannot make use of modern medicine and expertise to improve that one thing that is killing our self-belief? And if you don't, I can guarantee you that your friends and rivals *are* doing something to eliminate theirs. So don't be left behind!

Have a think about those elements of your physical appearance you could improve and write them down. We all have them. They could be very obscure things as well, for example, I used to have an extremely runny nose. I used to have to blow my nose every few minutes. Imagine being around somebody that has to do that, and naturally it made me very paranoid about what people were thinking about me. So what did I do? I dealt with it! I had an operation on my nose to stop the transparent fluid from streaming down every few minutes. Immediately afterwards, that whole barrier from my life was removed. It made me feel a lot better about myself not having to blow my nose in front of everybody every few minutes. Simple and effective!

Over the last ten years I've worked on a tonne of things I wasn't happy about. Each little thing took me that bit closer to where I wanted to be. I'm not talking about plastic surgery, that is completely unnecessary but there are many things you can do to improve your appearance and by default your confidence. You need to think what it is you're unhappy about and then do something about each one of them.

Let's take a look at two of the most common confidence killers that many of us will be able to relate to.

Bad Complexion

This was a major one for me as I was growing up. As soon as I hit 17 the spots and acne decided they were going to turn my life into a complete misery and they persisted for several years. If you are affected by this then I know it can ruin your life if you allow it. I was on internship wages at the time (£35 per week) and at least half of that money would go on creams, lotions, witch hazel sticks, ointments and prescribed remedies to treat my skin. I even once tried a homemade recipe which I remember contained paprika. I would smear this paprika paste all over my face before I went to bed. I would arrive at work the next day and people would ask why my face was stained orange. I even once went a full month washing my face once every hour to clean away the sebum; that just gave me a rash. I tried lots of things to try and improve my skin and get my confidence back.

One thing I noticed about all these "cures" is that many of them actually worked, at least for a short period before my skin became used to the treatment and would then become immune to it. This could happen in as short a period of time as two weeks; your skin becoming resistant to the treatments. You can now have special therapy that can clear up extreme cases but thankfully my condition improved before this was necessary.

One day I simply became completely fed up with spending the majority of my meagre wages on all these products that I just stopped, threw them all away and decided I was going to leave it to god. At the same time I started to drink a lot of water which is the main reason my complexion improved.

- Contrary to some beliefs, spots and acne have nothing to do with your diet or environment. It is completely down to genetics and most people are affected by this in their lives.

- Do not buy any product that aims to improve your complexion, they do not work and are a waste of money.

- Drink plenty of water. Aim for 6 litres a day, ideally you should always have your bottle of water on you. Take a short gulp once every 5 minutes. This is free and will have other health benefits for your body. Within a few weeks your complexion will improve dramatically and if you can stay in the habit of drinking water like I have, the effects will be permanent.

Seriously guys, if you have a bad complexion, water will do more good for you than anything else. The key is to take small amounts extremely often. You will be surprised at how quickly things will improve for you.

Bad Teeth

How many times have you seen an attractive girl only to see her teeth are not all that great? Wouldn't you agree that this is probably the one physical imperfection that would make the most difference to a person's looks? Girls are a lot less fussy about looks on men than we are with women. The exception to this rule though is with the teeth. I cannot emphasise enough to you the importance of having nice, straight white teeth. Don't believe me? Then ask any of your female friends how important nice teeth on guys are.

Teeth are one of the signs of a person's overall health, if your teeth are unhealthy, then so probably is the person they belong to. I really do hope that this section is something you won't have to spend much time and effort on (again, ask yourself honestly) in which case you should skip it. Ideally you should have had frequent trips to the dentist throughout your childhood and you should have great teeth.

If you have any missing teeth, overlapping, gaps or discolorment in there then you really should get them fixed. The vast majority of people shouldn't have any problems here but I personally know 3 people who have had complete replacement surgery carried out and it has improved their quality of life dramatically. If you are in the UK or the US then this can be very expensive. You can go to places like Hungary or Argentina to have this surgery carried out at a massively reduced price and have a holiday at the same time.

If your teeth are merely a little stained, as general life will make that happen then you can visit a dental hygienist who can truly effectively clean them up. You will be amazed at the difference a single trip to the dentist can make for the color of your teeth. From then on you only need yearly maintenance visits to keep them pearly white on a permanent basis.

Improve Your Posture

It should come as no surprise to you that our posture is an integral part of how we look and how others perceive us.

For many of us, having great posture is something we don't need to think about because we have it naturally anyway. However, for most of us, we need to be making a conscious effort to be upright when out and about.

In fact, scientific studies have now proven the link between our postures and our confidence and self belief.

It has been proven that when we sit up straight, with great postures, we have more belief in what it is we're saying.

Seventy-one Ohio State University students took part in a study, the purpose of which was kept from them. Instead, they were told they were taking part in two different studies, one to do with acting (holding various poses while doing other things), and one about business and job performance. They were asked to write down their best or worst qualities while they were sitting down with their back erect and pushing their chest out (confident posture) or slouched forward with their back curved (doubtful posture). Then, they completed a number of questions and reported their self-evaluations. These included evaluating whether they thought they were qualified or able to do certain jobs.

Confidence in what the students had said, good or bad, was significantly greater when students wrote their thoughts in the confident than in the doubtful posture. The students did not especially feel more confident in the "confident posture," but they did believe the things they had written more when they were in that posture instead of the "doubtful posture."

That means we are not even aware of our posture's influence on our confidence in what we say or write! Our posture directly affects how much we believe what we're communicating, and it's not just a matter of tricking ourselves by squaring our shoulders and "feeling confident."

In fact, the results were striking! How the students rated themselves as future professionals depended on which posture they held as they wrote the positive or negative traits. Students who held the upright, confident posture were much more likely to rate themselves in line with the positive or negative traits they wrote down. In other words, if they wrote positive traits about themselves, they rated themselves more highly, and if they wrote negative traits about themselves, they rated themselves lower.

However, students who assumed the slumped over, less confident posture, didn't seem convinced by their own thoughts – their ratings didn't differ much regardless of whether they wrote positive or negative things about themselves.

The author of the study says, "Most of us were taught that sitting up straight gives a good impression to other people, but it turns out that our posture can also affect how we think about ourselves. If you sit up straight, you end up convincing yourself by the posture you're in."

So you can see the clear benefits to our confidence in maintaining a good posture at all times, when sitting or standing. This is something we all need to be working on.

So how can you improve your posture? Well there are a few techniques you can use such as these below:

1. The balloon technique – While walking or standing, imagine there's a balloon on a string extending from the crown of your head. Imagine the balloon is pulling your head upwards towards

the sky. This will automatically make you stand upright with your spine elongated.

2. Keep in alignment – Try and keep your ears, shoulders and hips in perfect alignment when sitting. This will force you to sit up straight.

3. Pull in your abs when walking. This is perhaps the part where you're making the most effort, but also getting the most return too.

4. When sitting, keep the soles of your feet flat on the floor.

5. Be consistent – This means making a conscious effort to have great posture all the time. I know this can be a pain, but before long it will become natural.

Walk Faster

Next time you're in your local town, why not spend a few minutes people watching and see if you can tell who looks confident and who doesn't just from their walk.

Those who walk slowly always look to have the weight of the world upon them which never looks good or attractive. I can guarantee you that those who walk faster will appear more confident to you.

So why is this?

Well this is because we assume those people who walk quickly have somewhere to go, they have people to see and things to do. Basically, they look really busy even if they aren't.

It's true that you look on the outside to be really confident if you walk fast, we've established that, but how do they feel on the inside? We're going to talk more about exercise and its effects on confidence in a later section but since it's related to walking I'll also mention it here.

When you exercise or walk fast, your body releases endorphins which relax the body and calm the mind. This makes you feel good, even euphoric. I'm sure you can relate to this if you go to the gym, you'll already know you feel more confident every time you step outside after a good workout.

We walk every single day of our lives. So we should be taking these opportunities to walk a little bit faster than normal to release more of those endorphins. In the process we'll even look on the outside to those watching us to be more confident.

Try walking at a pace that's around 25% faster than what you normally would do. This should be fast enough to be overtaking the slow people around you. Try and have a natural and totally unforced swing of the arms in the process.

Another thing you should be doing while you're out and about walking is to smile. Smile and make eye contact with all the women you pass. Never be the one to break the eye contact. You'll find that if you make eye contact with women as you walk and then smile, many of them will smile back. Really, not many guys at all do this, and you'll stand out and seem really confident to the ladies. You'll also get a huge boost every time you get a nice smile back. Try it!

Remember also to have good posture while you walk. This means shoulders back and head up.

Smile And Make Eye Contact

I almost didn't include this section simply because it's so obvious; the majority of us know this already.

However, I decided to include this section because even though most of us already know about how positive smiling and making good eye contact with people is, we don't do it often enough.

This is especially true with smiling. A smile is one of the simplest and most effective things we can do. A simple smile makes us and everyone we interact with feel better. We radiate an inner peace and empathy that makes us instantaneously more likeable and approachable. A smile informs everyone around us that the world is not getting us down.

Smiling also affects the quality of our voices. Don't you think you're able to tell if someone is smiling when you're speaking to them on the phone? Of course you can! When you smile you sound a lot more friendly and approachable.

So remember to smile!

And now onto eye contact! Have you ever spoken to somebody who isn't looking at you while you speak to them? What impression does this give off?

It gives off the impression they don't care about you. But also it can give off the impression of inferiority.

Powerful people are not afraid to look into the eyes of the person they're speaking to. If someone fails to look into our eyes when they're speaking to us, it's interpreted as a lack of confidence and even an admission of outright inferiority.

I'm sure you've had a moment in your life where you've been stared down by somebody who's trying to assert their authority and superiority over you. I'm not saying you ought to go this far, but simply to understand the power and subliminal messages you give out by using good eye contact.

If you're in conversation with somebody and you're uncomfortable with prolonged eye contact then there's nothing wrong with breaking it for a few seconds, but you should always return to looking at them in their eyes. This will show you're comfortable with the person and confident.

Be Expressive Through Facial Expressions

It is said that when we speak to people, the words we actually speak account only for 10% of the overall message. While body language accounts for well over half, the exact number is debated.

There are two main aspects of body language which we'll be covering in this chapter and the next. Firstly there are your facial expressions and secondly there is your actual body language.

If you're curious what makes up the rest of the pie while we're speaking, it's a mixture of eye contact and smiling which we've already covered, voice tonality which we will cover in a bit and how you're actually speaking which we'll also cover.

The next time you're speaking to the people around you, take note of their actual facial expressions. What do you notice? I'm guessing you'll notice that not many people's facial expressions actually change while they talk. Most of us tend to keep a normal and straight face while we're talking to people. What message does this put across? Well it says you're not very interested in the conversation for one, but it also shows a lack of confidence.

The next time you're watching TV, take note of newsmen and TV presenters and watch their facial expressions while they talk. These people are the masters of the facial expression. They have to be! They got the job because they're able to draw people in primarily with their faces.

Watch a movie tonight and watch the actors and how they use facial expressions to convey passion, interest, humour and a whole host of other emotions.

This is just one of the reasons why people on TV always come over as being super confident.

You need to get into the habit of showing your emotion and interest in people when you speak to them by using expressive facial signals. In all honesty, not many people do this out in the real world and by being one of the few who do, you'll stand out for sure.

Practice talking in the mirror, don't laugh, I mean it, it'll be a great exercise for you. You need to get the balance right so that you don't look like you're overdoing it but instead it should come over as being completely natural.

This is so easy to do and it'll make such a huge difference to how confident you're perceived by others.

Body Language

Out of everything in this book, having confident and relaxed looking body language is perhaps the easiest and quickest thing to master in order to raise yourself up a few rungs on the confidence hierarchy. Whole books have been written about body language, it really is a huge area. Through body language, you are more able to show your confidence than through all other forms of communication put together. It really is crucial to becoming a more confident person, or at least being perceived by others as well as feeling it yourself that you master confident body language.

In fact this is a clear example of life imitating art. When looking around certain rooms, you can sense who appears confident through their body language. Usually those confident looking guys are the ones who appear most relaxed. But how do you know they are actually really confident people? They could have read this book and done everything I said in order to look confident, even though they may not be. But the truth is that you can alter people's behavior (confidence) on a temporary basis simply by modifying their positioning (body language).

You can easily tell a confident person just by looking at their body language. But did you know it's even possible to become more confident and more open simply by using body language to your advantage?

When you're speaking to people while your arms are crossed, you will naturally feel more defensive. However, if you actually drop your arms by your sides, you will actually feel yourself becoming more open and friendly. This works incredibly well! Likewise, you can also open up the front of your arms to people to create a similar effect.

I'll let you into a little secret. I used to be a dating coach a few years back before I took to writing informative guides for men such as this one. I used to teach a very powerful technique to the guys to help get women to open up to them and start being more friendly. I taught my clients that while they were on a date with a girl or if they were chatting to a girl in a bar and she had her arms folded then they could simply unfold them by complementing the girl on something and then giving her a high five. The girls arms almost never returned to the folded position and the girl would always open up and become friendlier. There have been many studies published that confirm this and more, that our body language actually commands how we feel in the moment and can therefore alter our state confidence.

I hope I've demonstrated that while yes, confident people will use more active body language, but it's equally true that by using active body language, you'll feel more confident as well. This is what I mean by life imitating art.

I recommend that you watch TV presenters and actors and mimic how they use body language. Try and gauge the correct amount to use, as it actually can be quite easy to overdo it if you're not careful. If in doubt, practice in the mirror.

So let's have a look at some examples of positive body language which you should be using:

1. Hand Gestures – You can easily practice your hand gestures in the mirror. This really is simple to do yet easy to overdo so try and strike up a balance. Simply bend your arms at the elbow when you speak and make slow gestures with your hands. You can increase the movement and intensity when you make a point in order to emphasize it. If you do feel yourself becoming nervous while you speak, especially if you're making a speech in front of a large group of people, one thing you can do is steeple your hands. This shows power and confidence which will certainly mask any nerves. Watch how politicians steeple their hands; it's an indicator of who the leader is.

2. Take Up Space – Confident people aren't afraid to spread themselves out a little. Next time you're in a meeting, spread your papers out around the table, move your coffee cup to the edge of your personal area. When you're sitting down, spread your legs out a little bit. Don't be afraid to prop your arm over the head of the chair next to you. This shows dominance and confidence. Think about how you lounge about the house when you're at home on the sofa and there's nothing there to alter your state. You feel relaxed, which is why you look relaxed and vice versa. Try and imitate this to a degree when you're out, at work or in a bar. When standing up, spread your feet out a little more to take up more of the floor area. This will give your body as well as your mind a "firmer footing."

3. Keep Your Movements Slow – Always be slow and controlled. Confident people are the exact opposite of erratic. Everything they do is calm, slow and deliberate. This shows you're in control of your body and there is nothing out there that can intimidate you. This should also include your hand gestures as described above, which should also be slow and comfortable.

4. Lower Your Drink – The majority of people keep their drinks close to their chest at all times. Similar to having folded arms, this acts as a barrier between you and everybody else. We do this for

protection because we are nervous or uncomfortable. Always lower your drink and keep it by your side. Confident people are open and don't need a wall between themselves and the people they are in the same room as.

5. Hand Shaking – When you shake someone's hand, do so with a good firm grip to show you're a real man and not a wet blanket. Another thing you can do to show your confidence is to give the other person a pat on the shoulder with your free hand. This is a subtle way of saying "I'm in charge here!" Just be careful you don't do this at a job interview. Notice how politicians and world leaders especially always pat each other on the back when they're instructing one another, leading them around etc. As a general rule of thumb, the guy who gives the final pat on the back to the other guy is the guy in charge. Did you see how Barack Obama and Mit Romney were patting each other hard and repeatedly on their backs during the presidential debating events? Finally, there was an extremely famous occasion in the Middle East where two politicians refused to walk through the door first because they each wanted to pat the other guy on the back as he walked through. Not to mention that neither wanted to be patted on the back by the other guy in front of the TV cameras.

Use with caution to show you're a confident guy, but just as importantly; realize when others are doing it to you.

Now let's take a look at some negative body language traits you should try and cut out:

1. Fidgeting – This is a big one and something all of us do unconsciously. We fidget mainly because we're nervous. Nervousness just happens to be the exact opposite of confidence so I suggest you try and consciously cut nervous traits out of your being. Simply by incorporating the positive body language traits mentioned above into yourself, you'll feel more confident anyway and fidgeting should automatically be reduced on its own. However, if you have any nervous ticks or you tap your fingers or feet then you must try and stop doing this. Do you often play with your cell phone just to give your hands something to do? This is fidgeting! Do you often take small sips of your drink for similar reasons? Try and cut this out. Do you touch your face or cover your mouth when speaking. This shows nervousness in a big way and that you don't actually believe what it is you're actually saying. Liars cover their mouth when they speak without even realizing it.

2. Don't Cross Your Arms – We've already covered this! By folding your arms you are creating a wall

between yourself and everybody else. This shows insecurity and discomfort. On top of that, it actually makes your whole attitude feel closed and shut off. Try speaking to your friends with your arms folded and then feel the difference when you unfold them, thus opening your body up. It's funny how things work sometimes.

3. Don't look down – This goes for when standing, sitting or walking. Looking down at the floor conveys weakness; defeated people look down. By holding your head up, you are exposing your neck, which evolutionary speaking is an extremely weak area. Therefore you are showing dominance by looking up because you don't expect any predator to dare make an attack on your weak and unprotected spot. Notice how Superman always looks up. He knows nobody is going to attack him and for good reason.

4. Don't react too quickly – Confident men are supposed to be calm. Nothing gets them worked up, hot and bothered. If somebody calls to you then don't snap your head looking around for who it was. Be slow, calm and controlled. Whenever there's panic in a room, notice how people always look towards the guy who's sat there unreactive; the calm person.

Voice Speed And Tonality

The speed and tonality in which we speak together make up the rest of how we are perceived by others while communicating. The speed you speak at and your tone of voice together are actually a lot more important to showing how confident you are than what it is you're actually saying.

Once again, I'm going to ask you to pay close attention to TV presenters and news anchors to learn from the masters.

Voice tonality in particular can be used to great effect. By alternating your pitch you will come over as being extremely interesting simply because practically nobody does it. You can use voice tonality to emphasise points and a lot more on top of that. The best way to describe how you should aim to sound is by saying you should talk with emotion. If you'd like to hear a great motivational speaker who can draw you in through voice tonality then watch a few Youtube videos featuring Tony Robbins.

With regards to speed, I'll say you should speak in a slow, calm and controlled way. By speaking slowly, you're showing your dominance and confidence. Have you ever spoken to somebody who speaks really quickly? This always makes them come over as being nervous and even erratic which clearly is not good.

In general you should always try and speak slowly and calmly however I'll also say that in order to sound a little more interesting, there's nothing wrong with alternating your speed a little bit just like you should be alternating your pitch. However, don't overdo this and use your best judgement. Think Brad Pitt in Fight Club!

I was advising one of my friends on voice speed. He is one of those who stops people in the street to sign them up to a charity. His problem was that people kept on walking away from him when he spoke, a big problem for many of these street charity people. When I saw him in the street working, I told him his problem was that he was speaking too quickly and he'd have more success if he slowed down a little. Because he spoke really quickly, he gave off the impression that what he had to say was not important and that speaking fast helped to get his message over before people had the chance to run away. He confirmed to me that this was why he spoke quickly. When I told him to slow the speed he was speaking at he told me he was afraid people would get bored of him and the end effect would still be the same. I made him realise that those thoughts were killing his confidence. Together we practiced his message in a more slow and controlled way. The results? Over the next week he had an increase of around 50% in signups.

Why was the increase so dramatic? Because by speaking slower, you are demonstrating complete confidence and belief in what you're saying.

As I mentioned earlier, if you adopt these confidence strategies into your being, you will actually feel real confidence within yourself. This will then further perpetuate more confidence from you. It's a positive spiral that all begins by learning all the above methods that help you appear confident on the outside, that will of course make you feel confidence on the inside.

Build An Attractive Figure

"To lose confidence in one's body is to lose confidence in oneself"

Simone De Beauvoir

Building a good body by working out can have an incredibly positive effect on your overall confidence in a number of ways. Firstly you have short term confidence and second you have long term confidence. We'll discuss both of these in this section.

Studies show that short term mood is lifted in the hours immediately following exercise. I'm sure you've noticed this yourself when you leave the gym you always feel a heck of a lot better than when you enter. This is because your body has been producing those endorphins which we mentioned earlier. Endorphins serve to lift your mood, calm you down and give you a feeling of euphoria. This can easily be interpreted as acute confidence which will last for a few hours after your session.

By going for a good workout every morning, you're setting yourself up for being in a good mood for the rest of the day.

The long term benefits on confidence from building an attractive figure are more obvious.

If we look good then we'll feel good! This will constantly be reinforced by society in how others look at us and treat us. After all, don't we as men look at women who have nice figures? This constant approval we're giving to women serves to reinforce their self image. You'll be glad to know it works both ways.

It has been proven that attractive people are more likely to have successful outcomes to job interviews. It has also been proven that attractive people are more likely to be promoted within their existing company structures. This is because we take attractive people more seriously than their non gym attending counterparts. It has even been shown there is a correlation between height and salaries with taller men being able to attribute every inch in height to an extra $600 a year in income.

Studies have shown that in court, attractive people are found guilty less often than their beer bellied counterparts and even when found guilty, guys with attractive figures receive a much more lenient sentence.

Is it any wonder people who have attractive figures are more confident individuals when society constantly tells them that they're attractive and desirable? Is it any wonder physically attractive people are more confident when society keeps on giving them helping hands like this?

In addition, when we know we look good, as guys, we're going to be more confident anyway! That's just the way it is and how it will always be!

Finally, when we go to the gym, we set goals for ourselves. Goals we like to achieve such as can we knock 20 seconds off that 10 km run or can we do 6 reps on the bench with a heavier weight. When we achieve these goals, we get a huge sense of accomplishment which makes us feel invincible.

This is not a keep fit or weight loss book. However, being physically fit is so important to confidence, I'm going to include a small section on the world's greatest ever fat killing technique that surprisingly few people even know about:

HIIT = High Intensity Interval Training

If you are overweight, or feel you could lose just a little bit of fat, then by far the best method of training is HIIT. HIIT stands for High Intensity Interval Training and there is a book by James Driver on that very subject that will quite possibly change your life.

Why does HIIT work so well? It is because it is intensive! When most people go for a run, they do so at an intensity of around 70% for an average of 45 minutes. Coming from an evolutionary perspective, no animal ever evolved due to stress at 70%! It takes a lot more than that. HIIT involves short bursts of all out sprints at 100% of your maximum intensity, followed by periods of walking. The walks are easy which makes the all-out sprints tolerable and even fun. But because you are giving your body more stress, the body makes much greater and much faster changes and it will do so in only a fraction of the time of a normal 45 minute jogging session.

Seriously, if you take any of my advice from this book, you need to invest in HIIT by James Driver. It is the single most superior cardio training method in existence and it will strip the fat from your body in no time. It will also increase your physical fitness; give you a greater level of endorphins (since they are synthesized as a response to pain i.e. from sprinting at 100% of your maximum intensity) and achieving that dream body in the shortest time possible will severely boost your confidence.

Drink Lots Of Water

Now, this section may sound a bit odd to you but hear me out. And don't worry, we'll keep it short.

Water has many benefits to the body and mind which I'll list for you below:

1. Water improves your skin and complexion

2. Detoxifies

3. Helps with our metabolism...

4. ...which can help with weight loss and keeping us fit

5. Keeps us alert by preventing tiredness

6. Prevents dehydration...

7. ...which can prevent headaches

8. Helps you think clearly (your brain is 90% water)

9. Regulates body temperature so you'll feel better when exercising

10. Water improves your mood

Seeing all these listed above, I can probably say that at least 5 or 6 of them can help with improving your confidence.

I for one can certainly testify to water improving your skin and complexion as I've already stated. And just in case you skipped the part above (my story about staining my face) I'm going to reiterate it here.

I used to have terrible acne in my early twenties. I used to spend a lot of money on all kinds of skin creams and lotions and none of them worked. This was all really ruining my confidence back then.

One day I kind of just flipped out and decided to stop wasting my money on these stupid creams that never worked. Heck, one time I even tried a home made concoction that contained paprika. For those of you who don't know, paprika is a bright orange or in some cases red herb. This stuff actually ended up staining my skin for a few weeks. If only I was kidding about this, although clearly I'm making light of it now.

After this, I was finally advised to drink more water. I put down all my fizzy drinks, teas and coffee and instead I drank only water. The way I did it was to always have a full bottle with me and I'd take regular small sips, probably over a hundred a day. I went through on average 8 or 9 x 500 ml bottles daily.

Within weeks, my skin was next to perfect. It was as if the answer was there all along and best of all, it was free. Water was the miracle that gave me back my beautiful skin which is why I decided to include water in this book.

Having bad skin can seriously damage your confidence and self esteem and can keep you locked in your room for months on end. I've been there! Please, if this sounds like you, the answer is to drink more water. Not only will it improve your skin, but it will have many other great physical, mental and emotional benefits for you as well.

Now my skin is superb again (all thanks to water), I can drink all the tea and coffee I want and the water more than takes care of the caffeine. This is lucky since I really enjoy tea and coffee. Who doesn't?

Be A Leader

There are many articles out there on being the so called alpha male but I'll break down briefly what traits alpha males have before getting into leadership.

In fact most of what I've covered already in this book has to do with being an alpha male; not caring what people think of you, dressing well, having good posture, walking with a purpose, spreading yourself out, being busy, using good eye contact, being expressive when you speak to people and using good body language (extremely important).

However, the most important alpha male trait of them all is being a leader!

Leadership is an extremely attractive trait! Being a leader is desirable in climbing the career ladder and also for having success with the ladies. Leadership ability is one of the most important reasons why *certain* people get promotions at work in front of those others who are less able to lead or organize. Organizing ability is valued. Having the ability to instruct other people and to get the best out of them will give you much better prospects throughout your career.

One of the main reasons the ugly guy is often able to get with the good looking girl is because he's an alpha male and because he's a good leader.

So what is leadership? Well when it comes down to it, leadership just happens to be the ability to organize.

Think to your social group. Who is the alpha male of your group? Is it by any chance the guy who carries out all the organizing? Is it the guy who calls up everybody and tells you all when and where you're meeting? My bet is that it is! Notice that he doesn't ask you all if you're meeting at a certain place at a certain time; more likely he actually tells you.

Every group, has to have a leader otherwise nothing will happen; the group dynamic will simply cease to exist. There has to be somebody who organizes and tells everyone where to be and what they're doing. This is true no matter how large or small the group, no matter what genders make up the group and no matter what the ages of the people in the group are. This is also true no matter where in the world you are or in what age or era you live in.

So what I suggest to you is that you should simply get into the habit of taking care of your own organizing. Start making plans for the group and give your friends the choice of joining in with what you're doing.

There is nothing magical about being the leader in any one group. But it does involve a conscious effort to lead. You'll need to organize your group meetings, you'll need to lead your group around the venue while you're together and you'll need to be the one to call it a day or night.

This is what confidence is!

Before long, this should appear natural to you and everyone will naturally assume you to be the leader.

The next time you're on a date with a girl, it's extra important that you lead! In fact this is imperative as leadership, as I've already stated is such an attractive trait in men for the ladies.

So what else does leadership involve?

Well, in the animal kingdom, being the alpha male of the group means you're the one in charge of protecting the group from danger. If there are any outside threats while you're out with the group, it'll be down to you to protect everybody. Do you think you can handle that?

In the animal kingdom, if the alpha male's status is challenged by a lesser male, they will fight it out. If the lesser male wins the fight then a new alpha male is declared and he is the one who gets first choice of women. He is the one who gets to lounge around in the shade while the lesser males go off to gather food.

Of course, this is all rather primal, but I hope I've got my point across to you. I'm not asking you to get into any fights to protect your group, but as the leader of your group, the others will certainly and instinctively look to you to deal with any threat from the outside.

Let me give you an example and switch genders here at the same time (not literally). Picture three girls at a bar chatting to each other. There is one girl, the pretty one that you want to talk to. Now it's odds on this girl isn't the alpha female, so you'll need to get the alpha females permission in order to speak to her. If you've read The Game by Neil Strauss, you'll have an idea of what I'm talking about. So how do you know who is the alpha female so you can go up to the group and start talking to her and thus fly in under the radar in order to speak to the one girl you actually want to speak to? Simple! She'll be the girl who'll speak for the group when you speak to all three of them with your opening line. She'll be the girl the other two instinctively look at in the expectation she'll speak for the three of them.

What the alpha female or Mother Hen is doing is protecting her flock. Switching back to being men again, this is something you'll have to do too.

Oh, and just so you know; you only need to be speaking to the Mother Hen for a short period, long enough for her to be comfortable with you before you can bring the girl you really want to speak to into the conversation. However, if you're doing this kind of thing out in the real world then I'm not sure why you're reading a book on gaining confidence.

So this yoga class you attend every Wednesday or this running class you attend every Thursday; who is the guy, or girl who organizes the social events? Who is the person who tells everybody else the class is getting together for its first ever meet up outside of class to get to know each other a little better?

Nobody I hear you say?

Well then this could be your chance to establish yourself as the organizer, the leader, the alpha! The confident one!

You should hopefully and ideally have already established yourself within the group and so organizing a night out for a few drinks, or a meal at a nice restaurant should be fairly straightforward for you to accomplish.

Don't wait around for somebody else in the group to organize a gathering. You must take the initiative to do it yourself. After all, that is what everybody else is waiting to happen. They are waiting for somebody else to organize an outing to make more interesting their lives. You need to be this person!

Have belief that you can do this and you'll surprise yourself. Remember that people are sociable creatures. They need human interaction and you're going to give them it!

When deciding where to go or what to do, the best thing you can decide is to do the one thing that benefits *yourself* and the *group* as a whole. You'll never please everybody all of the time, but you can certainly please the majority. In order to please the majority of people you'll have to have a think about what the majority of the people in your group likes. This could be fairly easy depending on what your group is; yoga, work, Italian cooking class etc.

Then when you have a good idea of your chosen activity, be *decisive*! Confident men are decisive! Don't ask what they would rather do; go to the new Italian restaurant in town or to the new Indian restaurant. Say that there is a new Italian restaurant in town and you are setting up a meal for the group. If you take away any choice or responsibility for the group members then you decrease the chances of non-compliance, or in this case, not showing up. This is because most people by their nature are followers and not leaders so if you give them work to do (making up their minds) then most people will simply defer to you anyway. However, you are a confident man, you have already put thought into it and you've decided for everybody that the new Italian would be great for everybody. If nobody has any thought (work) to put into the decision and you are decisive then you will get many accepted invitations.

Remember what I said at the beginning about making yourself uncomfortable, pushing yourself out of your comfort zone in order to expand it? Now is your chance to do just that!

"Practice Makes Perfect!"

Vince Lombardi

Expose Yourself (not literally)

By the title, I don't mean you need to run down the street naked in order to gain confidence. By exposing yourself I mean you should be doing little things every day that makes you uncomfortable.

When we try to build our muscles, we have to stress them as much as possible. Well to build our confidence we need to stress our minds.

I want you to ask yourself where you usually sit when you go to the coffee shop, or to a bar or anywhere for that matter.

Do you do what the vast majority of people do and sit in the corner, as long as that spots available? If not then do you head straight for the edges, keeping your back to the wall in order to feel safe and secure?

Answer the question honestly.

It's human nature to want to feel safe and secure and we can do this by protecting our rears. I can only assume this human trait came from when we all lived in the wild and we had to keep an eye out for predators such as Lions, Tigers and Komodo Dragons.

Millions of years of evolution later and this is still programmed into our DNA even though we know a Komodo Dragon is not going to creep up behind us and try to bite at our feet.

Why not live your life on the edge a little bit and next time you visit Starbucks take a seat in the middle of the room completely exposed to the eyes and glances of everyone around the edges.

Just think how confident this will make you look and feel to everyone else in Starbucks.

Next time you're standing in line, open up a conversation with some random stranger. Practically nobody does this as it's seen as taboo to speak to strangers, so you'll stand out a lot.

Next time you're at college or university, sit at the front where the lecturers typically pick on you. Volunteer to answer questions or to express an opinion in front of everybody. If you don't do this regularly then you'll feel a change within yourself by speaking out in front of so many people and so often. You'll never have a better chance than at college to speak out and push yourself so much. You really should take full advantage.

Why not take things to the next level and volunteer to do some sort of public speaking at university? One of my friends, who was already very confident by the way, volunteered to show a crowd of prospective students around the campus giving a talk along the way.

The same techniques for body language still apply when you're speaking in front of large groups. In fact by applying those techniques and by speaking with passion you'll have their full attention. Try alternating your eye contact between everybody watching you. It'll give you quite a thrill.

If you're not a student then volunteer to speak out at work or in the office. If you don't have a job that has this kind of potential for you then you should look online for a local improvisation class. Basically improv is acting on the spot, on your feet and in front of a group of people. You will be given a subject to act out with a group and you will play a role within that group. There are few things in existence that will build up your confidence better than an improv class.

Speak In Group Situations

As a prelude to what you'll be doing later on, providing you carry out all the tasks in this book, you really should make an effort to speak in all group situations.

Never be like all the other guys who simply keep their mouths shut and make it look like they're not interested in who's speaking or what they're saying.

If you go to college or university then you'll never have better opportunities to speak out, ask questions and make statements to both small and large groups of people. You should take every opportunity you can to let your voice be heard. Likewise, if you're in office or business meetings then you should also take every opportunity to speak out. I know I've already mentioned this above, but it truly is important that you push yourself.

If you have a speech you need to make then the best thing to do is to prepare what you have to say first. If you have chance then you should also practice. Remember the tips above which will make you sound infinitely better and more confident.

Having notes is fine and don't hesitate to look at the notes. But what you shouldn't be doing is reading from a script as this is not really going to push you out of your comfort zone far enough.

Maybe you work alone, don't work at all and don't go to university. Perhaps you have few opportunities to speak out to small or large groups. In which case I suggest you join some kind of a local group or society. What is it you're interested in? Simply find them on Facebook and join up.

If you really want to push the boat out and maximise your chances at speaking in front of large groups then join your local drama group (or improv class). I don't think there's anything in existence that'll inject your bloodstream with liquid confidence quite as quickly as these.

Have complete belief in yourself and in what you're saying. This will give your words more energy and clarity. This will also prevent you from fumbling your words. If this does happen, then carry on as if nothing is happening. And remember above all to not care what others may be thinking about you.

Finally, you should take a look at famous speakers on Youtube and see how they do/did it. Tony Robbins, Sir Oswald Mosley, JFK and Winston Churchill can all really inspire.

Disagree With People

Disagreeing with the people around you is one of life's great pleasures, and that is how you should see it.

Nobody likes people who simply agree with them on everything they say simply because they think it'll make them more popular. Attractive women in particular are used to men agreeing with them on everything and it really does not come over as being sincere, attractive and certainly not confident.

One of the principle things that makes confident people stand out from the rest of the crowd is their ability to disagree with others. On the flip side, how is agreeing with people on everything, especially if you don't actually agree with it any way to live your life? What does that say about us if we agree with people even if we actually think the opposite?

You really should make the effort to disagree with your friends, family and peers whenever the opportunity arises. Just make sure it's sincere and you're not just doing it for the sake of it. You're not playing devils advocate here, you're trying to build your confidence.

Feel free to disagree on the small things and the big things and everything in between.

However, it's important to realise the difference between disagreeing and having an argument. The two things are completely different and you should remember that.

Arguments can blow up out of all proportion which is not the desired effect you're trying to make, whereas a disagreement is something that is done constructively within the context of a conversation.

Do it and enjoy it!

Speak To Somebody New Everyday

This is one of the most important things you can do! Next time you're in the check out queue at the supermarket or shopping mall take note of how many people actually talk to each other.

Heck, the next time you're at your local bar, waiting to order your drink, have a look around and see how many people are talking to each other. This is quite an eye opener considering you go to bars to hang out, meet and talk to people.

By speaking to new people every single day, you are taking the bull by the horns and forcing yourself to become more confident. Nervous people don't talk to strangers! This is something you'll actually enjoy, trust me!

No matter where you are; at the bus stop, the line at Subway, in the lecture theatre, in the cereal aisle at the supermarket you should always be making an attempt to be friendly and to make small talk.

Just pick something situational or functional; the weather, how late the bus is, the prices at the store, how studies are going, the new piece of equipment at the gym, what the time is, something in the news.

Try and get into a conversation with a stranger every single day. If you miss a day then make it a rule that the next day you have to get into two conversations or three conversations to make up for it. Once you get good and you can feel your confidence improving, try and prolong the conversation. Find out what they do for a living. You never know when you might need a good mechanic or painter and decorator.

Be genuinely interested in the people you talk to and meet every day and your confidence will flow in you like you've never known before, I guarantee it.

This isn't just about improving your confidence; this is about improving your entire life.

Expand Your Social Circle

This may sound easier said than done, but it really doesn't need to be as difficult as you may think.

The best and easiest way to expand your social circle is in fact to utilize what you already have. By this I mean that you should develop the friendships you already have.

Those old school friends you haven't spoken to in ages, why not get together and go for a drink with them? In the age of Facebook this really is so easy to do and there really is no excuse for not being the bigger man and getting in touch with your old friends.

I recommend you look up all your old school friends on Facebook and see how they all are and ask what they're doing with their lives now. Tell them you're going to be in their area later in the week and that you should hook up for a drink.

Do this with all your old friends one by one. It's easy!

Likewise, you can also do this with your old work or sports team friends.

If you're at college or university then make more of an effort with the people already around you. I know full well how often they all go out to bars and clubs, so simply go along the next time they're out.

What you should also do to push yourself out of your comfort zone is to try and make completely new friends too; here's a story:

One of the world's most famous pick up artists became well-known for his social proof innovations within the field. In fact it was not unknown for him to enter bars with 100+ women. With such a huge social circle, one can clearly make magic happen. It was his rule to never hit on any of the women in his entourage; he needed their trust after all for his true pick up method to come to fruition. Imagine the impact any guy who enters a club with that kind of social proof would have on the thoughts of the other women in there. He never needed to pick up any women or do any work to try and get anybody interested in him. All the hottest women in the clubs would always approach him, just to find out what all the fuss was about.

Many years after perfecting this strategy, which he called Entourage Game, he explained exactly how he was able to turn up at a bar on a Monday, Tuesday, Wednesday, Thursday, Friday, Saturday or Sunday evening with over a hundred hot women.

He simply created his own club for women, where he would show them round the best bars in town, with the promise of cutting the queue and walking straight in along with the promise of an awesome night out. I suppose arriving to any bar with a hundred women also granted him favors with management (VIP treatment etc). He did it all through Facebook. Visitors in town, desiring a night out could find his service and he delivered.

He showed leadership and it paid off for him!

Now, you don't have to create your own giant club for party goers; that was just an extreme example of what is possible. But everybody has hobbies! There is nothing stopping you from creating your own club or society within your own area and getting together with like-minded people; with you as the organizer and leader.

Whatever your hobby is in this world, you will be able to find people to hang out with whether it be surfing, poker, diving, swimming, running, clubbing, stamp collecting or something I've not even heard about.

In the age of Facebook it is easier than ever before to create groups of people with similar interests in and around the area you live. There is nothing stopping you from creating a Facebook Tennis Manchester group or a Boston Sprinting group.

Create the group > Meet up > Do your chosen activity > Organize social gatherings

Nobody is going to do it for you. You have to take the initiative, be the confident man and create it yourself. It's easy!

Cool websites other than Facebook you can use to find like minded people are:

Meetup.com

Couchsurfing.org

You should also remember my advice to you above. Once you've infiltrated an existing group or created your new group, you should take the initiative to lead and to organize a night out for everybody.

Remember that even in the age of the internet, the number 1 way of meeting women and getting into relationships is still through social circles.

Having a good social circle is also your chance to do some good with it and in the process become even more popular yourself.

What I suggest you do is act as a connector. This means you should always be seeking opportunities to connect two members of your social circle together should the need arise. For example; you have a friend who is in need of good nutritional

74

advice and is willing to pay money. It just so happens you're friends with a nutritionist. Well all you need to do is give your friend the nutritionists number and get her/him to call.

Congratulations, you've just become a connector, improved two people's lives and done some real good with your social circle.

Maybe somebody in your new Tennis group for your home town needs a qualified joiner and you just happen to know a joiner from your zombie enthusiasts group. I'm sure you get the idea.

You'll be surprised at how often these situations will arise to act as a connector so you should always be on the alert.

Besides, it's incredible how karma often repays you many times over for your kindness to the universe.

Build your social circle and watch your life change!

Write A Speech Of Affirmations

A speech of affirmations can be a truly powerful method of making your brain believe something about yourself. Affirmations are statements you make to yourself to have a positive effect on the neural pathways in your brain.

Affirmations are used by many people around the world to have positive effects on your thoughts, feelings and behaviours.

To put this in its most basic perspective, what you'll be doing is writing a statement of how cool and confident you are and then reading it to yourself over and over. Follow these tips to help your statement work better:

1. Keep your statement of affirmations brief so you can remember it.

2. Be focused and specific. So regarding confidence, say specifically what you want confidence in.

3. Don't be negative but keep it positive. So don't say "I'm not nervous" but instead say "I am confident!"

4. Be in the present tense! It's better to say "I am confident" rather than "I will be confident!"

5. Try and visualize yourself while you're saying it. Use graphic language to help with this.

6. Say it to yourself every day at least 20 times! And say it like you mean it!

Here is a short speech of affirmations you could use and repeat it to yourself on a regular basis:

I am the most confident person I know. Everybody loves me! I am confident with women and they love being with me. I am a confident speaker and the audience hears my every word.

There you have it! Make sure you do something similar, tailored of course to your own lifestyle. It really is very simple!

Write A List Of Achievements

Similar to your affirmations above, which can be used to great effect, you should also write down a list of your achievements.

Carry this list around with you and read it whenever you have a spare moment. This list should perk you up and let you know your life is on track and focused.

List your qualifications and skills, list your best physical features, list what your friends like the best about you, write down what you're better than other people at, your hobbies, what makes you more interesting as a person than the next guy?

Then on the other side you should write a list of the things you want to achieve in the future; a set of short, medium and long term goals.

What a list like this will do for you is to keep you focused and motivated.

Start with what you want to have done by the end of the year. Things like; have spoken to a new person every day, have made 5 cool new friends, become a qualified..., run 10 miles in under...

Then write your monthly goals which should be your yearly goals but broken down into small manageable steps.

Every time you achieve one of your goals you can tick it off. Keep this piece of paper in your wallet and read it often. It'll really serve to keep your life on track to where you want it to go.

I'm sure you've also read the quotes that are littered throughout this book. Pick your favourite quotes and write them down on the same sheet of paper.

Become An Expert On Something

This should be a longer term goal for you!

Becoming an expert on something means that you'll have the ultimate confidence, within yourself at least in this particular field. You should endeavor to become the "go to" man in whatever it is you do!

When you become the "go to" man, then people inevitably flock to you. You'll be invited to more events than you can possibly handle, get to meet more people than is possible and get to make a huge difference in the process.

It doesn't matter what it is, but choose something, something very small and niche if need be and learn absolutely everything you can about it. If your job doesn't allow you to become an expert in that area then think about what your hobbies are? If you like going to the gym then become an expert on cardio or weight training; whichever one you prefer the most. If you like surfing then you should endeavour to not just become as good at surfing as you possibly can, but also learn everything about the sport too so that you would be the perfect person to go to if somebody wanted to learn to surf.

So what else does becoming an expert on something do for you?

Well how many people do you know that are experts at anything?

I'm guessing probably not too many.

Let's say for example you're an expert on creating websites. How many doors will this open for you? How many people could you meet and help out and how much money could you potentially make?

Remember that whatever it is you choose to become an expert in, you need to read as much as possible on the subject but you also need to practice it too. You can read all you want on bodybuilding for example, but you're not going to look like an expert unless you actually hit the gym.

Being an expert at yoga for example would mean you could walk into any yoga class in the world and appear like a confident individual, even if you didn't actually consider yourself a confident person. By being an expert in your chosen activity, job or hobby you'll be able to go anywhere in the world and meet with like-minded people and you will still be considered an expert, which will of course make you appear confident; which will make you *feel* confident.

I have a friend who is one of the best people you'll ever find for creating furniture by hand. He can all on his own create from start to finish any type of wooden furniture you can think of. He plans out his projects on paper, buys the correct kind of wood, shapes everything to the correct specifications and puts it all together. If anybody wants anything made from wood, they know who to go to. He gets to meet all kinds of people through what he does and he also gets to travel teaching workshops and giving lectures. This is because he is an expert and people seek out experts.

If you don't have anything you're an expert in then don't fret. The truth is that the vast majority of people are not and never will be an expert on anything. This is what you should see as your medium term goal. So pick something you're passionate about and attack it with everything you have.

Another motivator for becoming an expert is that it has been proven in scientific studies that women highly value expertise. In a study by Clegg, Nettle and Miell in 2011, it was found that from a sample of over 200 visual artists, the more successful artists had more sexual partners than the less successful artists. Interestingly the same thing could not be said for the female artists. This is evidence that while men do not necessarily value expertise and talent, women certainly do!

A study by Aggleton and Baker et al in 2004 found that students of both genders who participated in sports had a significantly higher number of sexual partners than did those students who did not take part in sports. Most interestingly of all however was that within the athletes, a greater level of performance was a predictor for even more sexual partners.

Hasleton and Miller in 2006 compared female preferences towards creative poor men and rich uncreative men. It was found that those women at peak fertility preferred the poor creative men over their richer yet less creative counterparts.

There you have it! This is evidence that becoming an expert in a field, any field is advantageous and consistent with success. There are many more studies showing expertise in a range of categories; I simply picked out three. It really doesn't matter what it is. It stands to reason that if there is a room full of geeky chess players, computer hackers or World of Warcraft enthusiasts; it will be the most talented in these areas who will get the most attention.

There aren't shortcuts.

Merely direct paths.

Most people don't take them because they frighten us.

Things that look like shortcuts are usually detours disguised as less work.

Seth Godin

Find A Confident Role Model And Copy Him

We go through all our lives with role models, this doesn't change as we grow older.

We cling to our role models spirit, knowledge and the example they set for us. But as we move through different phases of our lives, our role models inevitably change.

The person you choose can be somebody famous or somebody close to you; perhaps a friend, family member or somebody you work with.

This person should obviously be confident but they should be confident because of the qualities they have as people and not because of how famous they are or how much money they have.

They should have accomplished something meaningful in their lives, something that should also mean a lot to you.

They should have qualities you admire whether; physical, spiritual, emotional or moral.

So where can you find good role models around you? Well the workplace is a great place to start. Do you know any conscientious, good natured, confident and goal oriented people that fit the bill at work?

How about with your hobby? What is that one thing you're passionate about? Whatever this is; hang gliding, surfing, diving, body building, cooking; you need to find positive role models in this sphere too. Don't forget that when you reach a certain standard, you yourself will become a role model for others.

Remember that our every day lives are filled with wonderful people who are selfless and giving and ask for nothing in return. We meet people everyday who could potentially change our lives if we simply took the time to learn a little about them.

Remember to keep your eyes open!

Empower Yourself With Knowledge

Knowledge is the greatest thing on earth! Life is one long search for knowledge. If you stop learning you stop living.

By learning new things you're gaining confidence through competence at a range of skills. You'll be speaking to other people who are knowledgeable about what you're learning and others will want to talk to you about it too.

You should always be willing to learn more. I suggest to you that you make a list of things you're interested in and give yourself a year to get knowledgeable about them.

Pick a country you like, there are many interesting countries out there; France, Italy, Spain for example. Learn their language, learn about their culture and their cuisine. Take a trip there and talk to the locals in their native tongue. Travelling is something the vast majority of human beings are interested in. Learn about a country and you'll be able to talk to many people with ease.

Learn a new skill, you'll never know when it'll come in handy. You could learn car mechanic skills simply from looking at books, the internet and by actually checking under the bonnet of your vehicle. A skill like this will save you many thousands of dollars or pounds throughout your life as well as open up opportunities to help others along the way.

Remember that country you want to learn about? Well you should pick ten dishes of that country and learn to cook them all from your own head. Everybody loves a good cook and by becoming proficient at this important skill you'll be setting yourself up for a life of happiness.

Always be willing to learn a little something about anything. You'll meet people throughout your life with a whole range of curious interests. You'll be better prepared to make that person feel special because you'll know at least a little bit about their passion.

Destroy Your Weaknesses

I have a perhaps not so crazy friend who many years ago realized he was a terrible dancer. Do you want to know what he ended up doing? He decided to become a professional dancer! Can you believe that? He decided to become a professional dancer, teaching dance classes to all ages simply because that was his weak area.

My friend sure destroyed his weak area by attacking it head on!

I'm not suggesting you go for a career in something you have absolutely no idea about and the above is perhaps more of an extreme example.

But there are many valuable skills out there which the vast majority of us will need throughout our lives and some of these skills we'll be no good at in the slightest.

Can you drive? If not then you should work on getting your license as a matter of priority.

Can you cook? If not then learn! Start with easy things and progress from there. How are you intending on going through life if you can't cook?

Are you spending thousands of dollars on car repairs? This is really annoying for most of us, so why not learn to repair your car yourself. You'll be able to save on labour costs which are stupidly expensive and you'll also save on parts, as mechanics always double up on parts too just so you know.

Are you in bad shape? Then becoming physically fit is one of the most rewarding and confidence boosting things you can possibly do. Set out a route for yourself and run it. Go for a run along this route every other day and time yourself. Try and knock a few seconds off this time every time you do it. Beating your old times always gives a mental boost and makes you feel unstoppable.

Do you have any addictions? Whether it be drinking, smoking, gambling, drug taking or anything else that is having a negative impact on your life then you should work to beat this.

Doing all these things will help you become a much better, more rounded and more attractive individual that people will want to spend time with. It really is worth putting the time and effort in.

Aim To Go High In Your Career

There are a great many women out there who list ambition as the number 1 quality they look for in a man. Ambition is an extremely attractive quality for us guys to have! There are many women out there who get into relationships with guys and then end it, citing lack of ambition as the reason for the break-up of the relationship. If the guy isn't going anywhere in his life, then she will reason that he will hold her back too. This is a shame but in many cases it's the truth.

Why not ask a few of your female friends if they think ambition is an important quality in a man. See what they say!

You should also ask them if they think they can sense if a man is ambitious simply by looking at him. The answers you get may surprise you.

Have you ever seen an ambitious man who wasn't also really confident? Didn't think so! The two often go hand in hand; they feed off each other. As we've already discussed, confident men go further in their careers simply because they're better able to get their ideas across, inspire the best out of others and to ultimately make the company or organization more money.

Ask yourself if you are an ambitious man!

It is so very important that you are aspiring for better things down the line and that you are not simply settling for your present position, no matter what it may be.

You may be reading this and thinking that you are already happy and settled in your work or that you can't possibly go any higher in your field. For example, maybe you are already an airline pilot, or you already own your own company. In that case, what are you doing to try and improve life for all airline pilots? What are you doing to grow that company that you own?

In the vast majority of cases however, I'm going to go out on a limb and assume that most guys reading this book are not in fact working in their dream jobs with a six figure income.

Let me tell you now that it does not matter what you are doing right at this moment in time! It does not matter if you are a student, if you work in some lowly office position that you hate, if you are on an apprenticeship, it doesn't matter if you work on a check out and it certainly doesn't matter if you work at McDonalds. All that matters is that you have a desire to better your position and you *are actively doing something to change it*.

Remember, that if you're not growing, you're shrinking because other people around you, those people who are going after the same promotions as you, they are all growing.

You need to make sure you are growing at a faster pace than everybody else.

Let's take a few examples, and we'll make it difficult for ourselves by taking a few extreme examples to demonstrate my point.

Harry is 19, he has worked at McDonalds for two years. Harry loves working at McDonalds and when he speaks about it, people can see this in him. You see, the difference is that Harry has a plan. McDonalds are investing in Harry to go to chef school. Every day, Harry works flipping burgers and serving customers quarter pounder meals. But three nights a week, Harry goes to college to learn how to become a chef. In his spare time he experiments with his own recipes at home and he tests them out on his friends and family and gets their feedback. When his parents invite friends over to the house, Harry insists on doing all the cooking and testing out his new recipes that he created on the guests. Harry is compiling a book of these recipes, which are all English classics. Harry intends to sell this book online and he even hopes to have the book published. Harry also intends to open up his own restaurant, he just needs to finish chef school first so that then he can quit McDonalds and dedicate all his time to his dream.

Suddenly, working at McDonalds doesn't sound so bad does it! Do you really think there would be many people that Harry talks to who would be put off by the fact he works at McDonalds after hearing the rest of his story?

Kieron works on the checkout at the local supermarket. He hates it but everybody has to work. What he really wants to do is to become an artist. He knows it's hard to get into, selling your own paintings for a living. He knows also that there are not many opportunities around for being a full time artist. So Kieron puts up with working on the checkout for the time being. However, on his days off, he volunteers at the local art gallery. This enables him to work within his chosen industry and gain valuable experience. He also gets to meet and learn from other people and other artists who are already doing what he wants to do. He is making contacts and connections. In his spare time he paints his pictures, expanding his portfolio. He has created a website for himself where he showcases his work and tries to make a name for himself. He attends as many art shows as he can get to and he is always trying to learn more and improve himself within his craft. Becoming a full time artist is very tough. But Kieron has a plan and every day he knows he is getting one step closer to achieving his dream.

What do Harry and Kieron both have in common? They both work in jobs that would put many people off wanting to get to know them better. But they both have a plan! An action plan that they are actively working with to improve their situations. Every day, they are getting just that little bit closer to achieving their dreams.

Ambition is an incredible quality to have! But actually having a plan and actually executing a little piece of that plan every single day is putting that ambition into practice. That is what makes all the difference.

Let's now take a look at Andy.

Andy is in his mid-thirties and had worked for a construction company for fifteen years before the company hit hard times and made Andy and several of his colleagues redundant. Andy is now unemployed. Andy hates unemployment, it's boring and soul destroying. All he's ever known is the construction industry and he knows the industry very well. Andy contacted several of his former colleagues who were also made redundant, those people who also know and love the industry and wish to remain within it. Andy and another four guys decide to sit down and come up with a plan together, to establish their own construction company. It's hard work because the economy is slow but every day the five of them are working towards building up this new construction company.

You see, even the unemployed can still go far, as long as they have ambition and drive.

But even ambition may not be good enough if you are doing nothing about that ambition. Once again, what sets Harry, Kieron and Andy apart is that they all have a plan, written down and they are working towards that plan. One day, they will all make it. There is no way they can't! None of those guys are blaming society, a lack of education, a lack of opportunity, lack of parental help or the fact they were made unemployed for their present position. All these guys have grabbed their lives by the balls and are taking *personal responsibility* for themselves and their position. If they have any failures or setbacks along the way then they will not blame the bank, the economy or anybody else. They will simply learn from it and move on a lot stronger than they were before.

Confident men take personal responsibility! By relying on other people, the council, the state or other outside forces for your situation; you are giving away all your power to improve your position.

These three guys will succeed and anyone who speaks to them knows this! They have ambition. They have confidence! They have confidence in their abilities! Women love guys who have ambition. It is far more attractive to have an ambitious guy than a guy who has already made it but who wants to progress no further. Those at the top can lose what they have very easily and if they lack that fire and ambition then there will be no way they can ever get back to where they were.

Just like Baz Luhrman said in the song Sunscreen: Never take a lover or a trust fund for granted – You never know when either will run out!

Remember: If you're not growing, you're shrinking because others are growing!

You need to decide where you want to be in life! Have a plan for ten years. Have a plan for 5 years. Have a plan for next year. Finally, as I've already stated; have a plan for each year broken down into manageable monthly segments that you can tick off as you accomplish them.

Actually, physically write down a plan on a sheet of paper and carry it around with you. Look at it every few days and make sure you are taking the measures necessary on that sheet of paper. When you complete them, tick them off.

Studies have shown that by actually having a written plan of your short term goals, you are more likely to achieve them. This is because you are making yourself accountable, to yourself! You are taking *personal responsibility*!

Hopefully you will already know what it is you want to do in life and what your dreams are. If that is the case then you can skip the next section.

What if you don't know what you want to do?

Clearly knowing what your dreams are so you can work towards them is imperative to creating your plan. If you have no idea what you want to be doing with your life then it's important that you take the time to discover it, so that then, finally you can dedicate everything towards getting there.

Take a look at these suggestions for trying to discover what you should be doing.

- Write down the five things you enjoy doing the most. If you have any hobbies such as playing music, drawing, writing or travelling then write them down. Which of the five do you enjoy the most and which of the five have the most viable career options?
- What are you really good at? Do you excel at anything? Do you speak a foreign language well? Is there any extreme sport you're good at? Do you have any special knowledge of any particular subject? Write them down. Are there any careers within this area?
- Are you an expert at anything? Do you have any prior knowledge from former jobs that would qualify you as an expert in a certain area?

- What hobbies have you always wanted to take up but have never gotten round to starting? Are there viable careers within these hobbies?
- What did you really enjoy doing at school? Was there any particular subject you were really good at?
- Imagine you just discovered you only have a year left to live. What do you regret never doing?

Discovering that one thing you want to dedicate everything towards is not easy, I totally understand that. But if you don't yet know what it is, it's very important you dedicate some time and literally have a deep think about what you want from life.

Only once you know what it is can you then go full throttle in that direction and dedicate everything you have to getting there.

Never underestimate the power of having this fire and ambition towards improving your confidence to the extreme levels of the stratosphere. There are few things that can give a man confidence more than the thought he is going places in life.

Whatever your chosen career path is, you should aim to go right to the top!

Cut Out Useless And Negative People

For many people, the reason they are so negative or nervous the whole time is because they are surrounded by people who are negative or nervous.

Moods are infectious. Laughter spreads as do smiles, happiness and generosity. Unfortunately this is also true of bad traits and emotions. Doom and gloom can spread throughout a room like wildfire and put you in a bad state of mind for the rest of the day.

Everybody knows people like this. People who from the minute you sit down with them start bad mouthing other people or start being critical of every little thing and in general put a downer on the mood, even if there's no real reason for it.

I'm sure that describes at least a few people you know and probably know all too well.

I'm not one to recommend you start cutting out your best friends, but if this sounds like a mood you're always in and have never known why then this could be the reason. If you have a negative friend then you should talk to him and tell him you're not willing to put up with his negativity and bad moods any longer.

If you tell your friend for example that you want to be a fireman and he laughs and says you haven't got what it takes then this person is seriously damaging your confidence.

Give him a final chance and if he doesn't change and it's dragging your mood down, then you need to do the kind thing to him and to yourself and cut him out of your life. You're only alive the one time so can you really afford to be around people like this if it's dragging your confidence and life down in the process?

On the contrary, you should find some positive, happy and already confident people to spend your time with. Feel how these positive qualities rub off on you. You'll soon notice that your days are spent much happier and it's having an incredible effect on your life.

Trust me, this is very important. You need to surround yourself with good, happy people who are also positive role models. This will make a huge difference to your confidence.

If you follow the advice in this book then you are going to find yourself becoming more confident, you're going to find yourself changing.

If the people around you suddenly start to find that you're becoming more confident, getting more attention from men, women and other groups, then it is highly likely they are going to feel left behind.

It is most likely your present peers will do one of two things: 1. They will be happy for you. 2. They will indeed feel left behind and envious of your progress and will be unhappy for themselves. Jealousy is the best word for it!

This also provides you with two options. Hopefully, you'll be able to take your friends with you on the journey and help to improve their lives too. This of course will mean that they will have to put work into themselves, put down the Playstation and embrace the journey. Friends that are happy for you when you are doing better than they are, are actually true friends who're hard to come by.

However, if they refuse to be happy for you, they are going to drag you down. You can't improve your confidence when you're still spending time with people who are bringing you down. There's no reason for a confident guy to put up with that kind of crap from anybody!

I hope you'll be able to stick with your old true friends as you start meeting many new people, in fact you really need to put in the extra effort for all those people who've always been there for you. However, you also need to be prepared to let them go if they prove to be a barrier between you becoming the guy you want to be.

People, women in particular tend to notice how those around us treat us and interact with us. You may be able to fake being a confident man, at least for a short period of time, but as soon as your new people meet your old people and see your interactions then that's how they'll know straight away whether you're the kind of guy they want to spend time with.

Do the people you know really well treat you with respect? Or do they talk down to you, bad mouth you, cause you problems and heartache?

If these people aren't going to shape up, then you need to drop them. Confident men do not need to put up with taking crap from people. You can't improve your life whilst old people are dragging you down and we all know people who would fit this description.

If they are dear to you then give them a final warning. Be confident, take charge and tell them straight. You are not going to take this crap any longer. Then if it continues, then you need to be willing to follow through with your word.

Before long, you'll be surrounded with high quality, high value people who in turn will raise you up a few pegs, as you will do for them. We are products of our environments, so we need to create those environments ourselves. Aim for excellence and nothing less. Create an environment for yourself that other people want to be a part of and you will find that people naturally gravitate towards you.

Know Your Principles And Live Them

This is the last section in this book for a reason and you should have a big think about what I say here once you've finished.

What are the principles by which you live your life? Do you know what they are? If not then you'll have trouble because your life will feel like it lacks direction.

Our lives require direction in order for us to be able to attack it with all we have!

Have a think about what your principles are and what you believe in. Are these principles important enough to you that you're willing to stand up and argue in their favour? If not then you should probably change them.

Now have a think about whether you simply believe in these principles but don't act on them or if you actually take account of these principles and live them.

What are your political beliefs? If you don't have any then don't you think you should? What are your spiritual beliefs? What is the most important trait in human beings you admire the most? Is it dedication, empathy, friendliness or passion?

For me it's dignity, which I define as "always being the bigger man in any given situation!"

What is it for you? Once again, is it important enough for you that you're willing to take a hit to defend it or to live it?

You'll find that when you have a set of principles and a set of beliefs that you're willing to stand up for, your life becomes a whole lot clearer, has direction and is so much more meaningful.

Are your principles steadfast? Or are they likely to change according to the current trends, the opinions of your friends and peers or of what the media deems is acceptable?

Having a set of core beliefs and principles with which to live by is the major keystone to knowing yourself and having confidence in the person you are.

"You miss 100% of the shots you don't take!"

Wayne Gretzky

Section 3

Living The Dream

"Life is very generous to those who put themselves on the line!"

Charlie Valentino

Experience Life

In this section I'm going to give you a few ideas of things you can do to change your life for the better. Unlike the last section where we dealt mainly with theory, principles and strategies to force confidence upon you, in this section I'm going to give you cool things you can actually do.

You're not going to be able to do very many of them, in fact I highly recommend you come up with your own. These are included as ideas for you and because I know they'll work to give you all you'll ever want.

Imagine doing these things and how you'll be able to talk to people and captivate them about how you've done them. That is because these things listed below are super cool and will make you a more interesting and by default confident person.

We gain confidence through our experiences so you should endeavour to experience as much as you can in life.

If you're unhappy with your life, if you want to make a change for the better, you need to think big and you need to be ready to put in the work to make it happen. It's easy to visualize success and to think positively; it's not so easy to throw yourself into the unknown and make it work. But if you can make it work, you'll gain far more than you can imagine.

One of the principle pieces of advice I give to guys to become more confident is to gain life experience. Many different and interesting life experiences!

Remember when I said we become confident in different areas through competence. Well by achieving enough competence in many different areas, one can reasonably expect to become a confident person throughout their life.

You know all those people who appear super confident because they're chatting away to all their friends about having gone sky diving over the weekend, or because they've just come back from a year away travelling, or because they have a cool story to tell about how they just got a girl's phone number, or because they've just stood in front of two hundred people and made a speech, or because they've just started attending drama classes, or because they've just climbed a mountain, or because they've just camped out in the wilderness, or because they've just cycled from one end of the country to the other or because they've just learnt how to hang glide.

What do these people have in common?

They are all getting out there and living their lives! They are having fun! They are meeting people! They are telling their stories! They are experiencing life to the full!

Certain guys appear confident because they have life experiences and they can draw people in partly because of this.

Everybody has a long list of things in their heads that they really want to get round to doing at some point in their lives. However, certain guys actually go out there and do these things! They don't sit back and think about it, they just get up and do it!

Confident men are action takers!

What are those things you have always wanted to do but never had the inclination to look in to? Write a list of those things, trust me, actually seeing them written down in front of you is the first step, having them in your head is not.

After writing them down, choose those activities that you can do *now*! Make a commitment to yourself to do them!

For me, the thing I always wanted to do was learn to breakdance! So I went out and did it! Many of my best friends are break dancers and I've had relationships with girls through that activity. What is your chosen activity? You will meet your best friends in life through hobbies that you share in common.

I didn't stop at break dancing however. I always wanted to learn Italian due to an obsession with that country, so not only did I learn to speak the language, but I also spent a whole month travelling throughout Italy.

Now I'm a little too old to breakdance any more so I am starting my own running class. Remember HIIT (High Intensity Interval Training) that I was telling you about? I am now starting a class in my area, three times a week where we do HIIT in the local park.

Imagine the stories I'll be able to tell new people I meet about running my own HIIT class, where I guarantee everybody who attends will lose weight faster than any other method. Imagine the amount of people I'll meet by running my own running class three evenings a week. As I mentioned earlier, we'll also no doubt be having frequent evening socials.

Last year I went out on my bike and cycled along the canal. I didn't stop until I reached the end...In Liverpool, 140 miles away! Then I cycled back. It took me a little more than a day and a night to complete. That's another life experience I can tick off the list and I could talk for an hour about the day I did that, the things I saw and experienced, the pain I felt.

If there's something I am interested in doing then I plan it out and I do it! I certainly don't waste time playing on the Playstation. I don't spend all my time in bed. I am getting out there and living my life.

I used to be the guy who hid my face behind my hair so I wouldn't need to look anybody in the eye and now I'm teaching running classes.

Now I'm the guy who appears super confident because I can hold a group of people with my stories about breakdancing, travelling, Italy, HIIT, doing spontaneous cycling trips and soon to be hang gliding.

It really is that simple!

Experience Life!

Get out there and take ACTION!!!

"We do these things, not because they are easy, but because they are hard!"

JFK

1. Approach A Woman On The Street And Tell Her She's Hot!

2. Do Some Public Speaking

3. Learn A Language And Take A Language Teaching Course At Source

4. Go Skydiving

5. Join A Drama Group

6. Go Travelling

7. Go Diving

8. Get Your Pilots License

9. Learn To Surf

10. Build A Website

11. Climb A Mountain

12. Go Camping In The Wilderness, Alone

13. Cycle Cross Country

14. Befriend An Enemy

15. Go Hang Gliding

16. Learn A Musical Instrument

17. Enter A Triathlon

18. Meet Your Hero

19. Enter A Tough Guy Competition

20. Start A Part Time Business

Final Words

If you've made it this far and taken in everything I've said, but more importantly put everything into action, you will become more confident. It's as simple as that!

It's all down to you now! You owe it to yourself to give it everything!

If you've enjoyed this book and you think others would benefit from the advice I give, then please leave an honest review on Amazon. I read all reviews and it would mean a lot. Thanks and good luck!

Also By Charlie Valentino

First Date Tips for Men

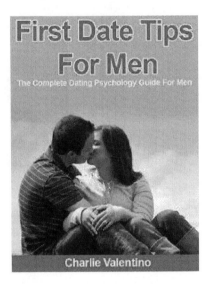

The complete dating psychology guide for men! - This powerful book gives men the ability to completely captivate women on dates.

There are many techniques and strategies in First Date Tips for Men, some practical, others logistical. However it is the psychological tips, the getting into the female mind, to have her thinking about you even after the date is over that really makes this book truly unique.

Here's a few of the things you'll learn inside:

- How to compliment her correctly to get her to open up to you.

- Establishing a connection. This will make her feel like she's known you a long time.
- Rapport breaking. This is powerful and will make her chase you.
- Qualification. This is the secret weapon. Few guys use qualification! This is how you stand out and get her to chase you for a long time.

If only I knew these things as a teenager!

Meet Women on Facebook

Meeting women on Facebook is easy, as long as you know what you're doing!

You need a profile that makes you stand out from the rest of the guys out there, who message random girls all the time hoping for a response.

Learn how to craft the best Facebook profile possible to enable picking up girls on Facebook easy!

After that, use our Facebook pickup lines to pique her interest and have her impatiently message you back.

It's all here in Meet Women on Facebook to make Facebook pick up easy for any guy out there.

No matter if she's an existing Facebook friend, a friend of a friend or you have no connection with her whatsoever, discover the complete formula from the first message to the first date now.

With most of the world's hot girls on Facebook, Facebook dating is the future! Don't miss the boat on this one!

Destroy Approach Anxiety – Effortlessly Approach Women without Fear

Approach anxiety is something the vast majority of aspiring pick up artists suffer from when starting out approaching girls. If we can't get over approach anxiety, our first major stumbling block in the world of pick up then we're not going to meet many attractive women.

Destroy Approach Anxiety covers this subject so you can get over this easily and then on to the good stuff which is approaching women without fear.

Find out the true reasons why we suffer from approach anxiety, it may surprise you. One of the author's beliefs is that it's the overloading of information in our heads in an attempt to gain perfection before we've even made our first approach. This is impossible!

The author emphasizes the importance of keeping pick up as simple as possible, especially when suffering from approach anxiety. He gives numerous strategies for maintaining the perfect pick up, without overloading the head with too much information, which you can't possibly act on when under pressure approaching hot women.

Destroy Approach Anxiety should be the first PUA book you read as it will help you find approaching girls in the street as simple as possible by getting you in the right frame of mind.

Direct Day Game Method – Pickup Girls on the Street, at the Mall or Coffee Shop!

Direct day game allows guys to cut the crap and just get to the point! It's just you and her in the moment! That's why it works so well, women respect guys who put themselves on the line! - Charlie Valentino.

There is nothing quite so empowering as being able to walk straight up to any girl in the middle of the street and tell her you think she's stunning! This is what Charlie has been doing for years and he shows you how you can do it too.

Using the direct approach on a girl during the day in the street, coffee shop, mall or university campus is about as straightforward as pickup gets. For this reason Charlie Valentino says it's the best method for beginners and newbies or for those suffering from approach anxiety. Because the direct day game approach for meeting women really does cut the structure of pick up right down to its bare bones. There will be no rubbish flying through your head, no lines, stories, routines, tips or tricks. It's just you and a very attractive girl in the moment.

Charlie shows you how it's done with ease and a high probability of success!

Online Dating For Men

1 in 5 new relationships now begin from an online dating site. Given that only a few short years ago this figure was zero, this is quite impressive. It is estimated that within a few years, the vast majority of new relationships will begin through meeting on an online dating site!

Having said that, 95% of all men who sign up to an internet dating site will give up within one subscription term.

Charlie Valentino has now authored his sixth relationship book for men, aiming to help guys meet their dream girl whether on Match.com, Plenty of Fish or any other online dating site.

In this book you'll learn:
- The mind set and strategy you must take to set yourself apart from all the other guys online.
- The pitfalls of online dating and why most men fail.
- The webs best online dating sites and which ones to avoid.
- All you need to know to create the single best profile that will stop women in their tracks. Crafting that perfect profile is the single most important thing you must do to ensure women return your emails. Charlie Valentino previously authored Meet Women on Facebook and is an expert on creating enticing online profiles.
- Discover the many mistakes that men make with their profiles so you can ensure you don't make the same mistakes.
- Learn how to craft the perfect opening email to send to girls to give yourself the highest possible chance of receiving a reply.
- Charlie also shows you his tried and tested cut and paste email system.
- See evidence of what 99% of guys are doing and why it's impossible for them to stand out and make any impact. This is valuable information to know, so you don't do the same.

Online Dating For Men contains all you need to know in order to attract women online, improving dramatically your chances of dating as many women as you like through online dating websites.

The Alpha Male System

The Alpha Male System

8 Elements To Becoming
Alpha Male!

Charlie Valentino

The Alpha Male System concentrates on eight fundamental alpha male elements which are visible as well as desirable in all leaders of men, which women also happen to crave in abundance.

In the days of the "metro sexual," men with alpha male traits and qualities are becoming rarer and increasingly more sought after.

Those few alpha males who can lead people, command respect and change the dynamic of a room simply by walking in it have all the luck. Or is it luck?

Discover the eight alpha male elements which will change your life along with detailed plans to attain them.

Becoming an alpha male is possible for most people, as long as you're willing to put a little work into yourself.

22396726R00083

Made in the USA
Lexington, KY
25 April 2013